To Yvonne,
Thank you for everything
you do for us.
With love
Viv, Chris and Ruth xx

Joy of Bears

SYLVIA DOLSON

Front cover photo by Sylvia Dolson
Back cover photo by Derek Kyostia
Book design by Fiona Raven

First Printing May 2013
Printed and bound in Canada by Friesens

Published by
Get Bear Smart Society
P.O. Box 502
Whistler, BC V0N 1B0
www.bearsmart.com

MIX
Paper from responsible sources
FSC® C016245

ENVIRONMENTAL BENEFITS STATEMENT

Get Bear Smart Society saved the following resources by printing the pages of this book on chlorine free paper made with 10% post-consumer waste.

TREES	WATER	ENERGY	SOLID WASTE	GREENHOUSE GASES
3 FULLY GROWN	1,509 GALLONS	2 MILLION BTUs	101 POUNDS	278 POUNDS

Environmental impact estimates were made using the Environmental Paper Network Paper Calculator 3.2. For more information visit www.papercalculator.org.

Library and Archives Canada Cataloguing in Publication

Dolson, Sylvia
    Joy of bears / Sylvia Dolson.

ISBN 978-0-9813813-2-9

1. Black bear—Pictorial works. 2. Grizzly bear—Pictorial works. 3. Polar bear—Pictorial works.
I. Title.

QL737.C27D635 2013   599.78   C2013-902292-9

....

CREDITS: *Best efforts have been made to find the original sources of quotes and obtain copyright permission.* Page 27: from *Second Nature: The Inner Lives of Animals*, by Jonathan Balcombe, p. 203–204, reprinted with permission from the author ❧ Page 28: first quote from *The Journey Home* by Edward Abbey, copyright © 1977 by Edward Abbey. Used by permission of Dutton, a division of Penguin Group (USA) Inc.; second quote from *Desert Solitaire: A Season in the Wilderness* by Edward Abbey, p. 167, published by arrangement with McGraw-Hill Book Company ❧ Page 73: from the book *Guardians of Being*. Copyright © 2009 Eckhart Tolle, Eckhart Teachings, Inc. Reprinted with permission from New World Library. www.NewWorldLibrary. com ❧ Page 78: from *A Joseph Campbell Companion, Reflections on the Art of Living* by Joseph Campbell, 1991, reprinted by permission of the Joseph Campbell Foundation (jcf.org) ❧ Page 98: from *A Return to Love: Reflections on the Principles of "A Course in Miracles"* by Marianne Williamson, p. xx *Introduction*, reprinted with permission from the author ❧ *Other quotes have been reprinted with permission of the author, publisher or their representative, but are not noted individually.*

Dedicated to Jeanie
1991–2011

Thank you for allowing us to share in your life; bringing joy to all those who were privileged to spend time in your company. You taught us about patience, tolerance and the depth of mother-love. You showed us that bears have unique emotions, quirks and personalities, and that perhaps we are more similar to bears than we thought. For that I will be forever grateful. This book of bear hugs is for you and for all those who do their part to protect your kind.

PHOTO BY SYLVIA DOLSON

4

For the love of bears

In almost 20 years spent photographing, studying and being in the company of bears, I have never ceased to be captivated by these magnificent animals. Sharing space with bears warms my heart, elevates my soul and gives purpose to my life.

I truly believe that this connection with wild animals in their natural environment brings a sense of harmony and joy to those who experience it. In this book, I am honored to share with you a few of my favorite images of bears, along with some poignant words of inspiration.

For every encounter I am blessed with and every moment I spend in their presence, I am grateful for the existence of the great bear. And with that gratitude ever-present, I commit to serving bears and other sentient beings, protecting them from harm, and practicing genuine compassion, caring and kindness.

I hope the images and words in this book permeate your heart in wonder, replenish your spirit and live within you to inspire you and forever bring you peace and joy. From my heart to yours, with gratitude for being a careful steward of our shared habitat, I thank you for being an ambassador for those who cannot speak for themselves.

Please join me in sincerely thanking those who shared their powerful words and the photographers who enthusiastically donated their photos to this project to celebrate bears – Nikolai Zinoviev, Michael Poliza, Derek Kyostia, Tony Dathan, Dennis Fast, David Krughoff, Deb Potts, James Fougere and Jamie Douglas. With gratitude to the Vancouver Foundation and the Community Foundation of Whistler for making it possible and to everyone who helped make this book special.

Let yourself be silently DRAWN
by the stronger pull of what you REALLY love ∾
Let the BEAUTY of what you love
be *what you do.*

RUMI

$\mathcal{W}$hen you are where wild bears *live*
you learn to pay attention
to the RHYTHM of the land and yourself ❧
BEARS not only make the habitat RICH,
they ENRICH us just by *being*.

LINDA JO HUNTER

8

PHOTOS BY SYLVIA DOLSON

*The question is no longer
DO animals think? But
WHAT do animals think?*

MARC BEKOFF

Bears keep me HUMBLE ∾ They help me
to keep the world in perspective and to
understand where I fit on the spectrum of life ∾
We need to **PRESERVE** the wilderness and its monarchs for
ourselves, and for the dreams of children ∾
We should FIGHT for these things as if our *life*
depended on it, because IT DOES.

WAYNE LYNCH

PHOTOS BY MICHAEL POLIZA

14

What is a man without the BEASTS?
If all the beasts were gone, men would die from
great loneliness of SPIRIT, for whatever happens to the beasts
also happens to man ❧
All things are connected ❧ THIS WE KNOW ❧
Whatever befalls the EARTH befalls the sons of the Earth
❧ Man did not WEAVE the web of LIFE,
he is merely a strand in it ❧
Whatever he does to the web, he does to *himself*.

CHIEF SEATTLE

*A*n animal's *eyes*
have the **POWER**
to *speak* a great language.

MARTIN BUBER

*B*e **KIND** whenever possible ∾
It is ALWAYS possible.

14TH DALAI LAMA

PHOTO BY DEB POTTS

Like us, animals feel love, joy, fear and pain, but they cannot grasp the spoken WORD ∾ It is our obligation to **SPEAK** on their behalf ensuring their well-being and lives are RESPECTED and *protected.*

SYLVIA DOLSON

20

PHOTOS BY SYLVIA DOLSON

PHOTO BY NIKOLAI ZINOVIEV

A problem for BEARS is not so much
what we DON'T know,
it's what we THINK we know that isn't *true.*

LYNN ROGERS

Animals have hearts that FEEL,
eyes that SEE,
and families to **CARE** for,
just like *you* and *me.*

ANTHONY DOUGLAS WILLIAMS

PHOTOS BY MATTHIAS BREITER

Animals are not just living things;
they are BEINGS with lives…
that makes all the difference in the world…
next time you are outside…NOTICE the first animal you see…
you are beholding a unique individual with personality traits,
an emotional profile, and a library of knowledge
built on experience…what you are witnessing
is not just BIOLOGY,
but a *biography*.

JONATHAN BALCOMBE

The idea of WILDERNESS needs no defense
∾ It only needs more defenders.

But the *love* of wilderness is more than a HUNGER
for what is always beyond reach;
it is also an EXPRESSION of loyalty
to the earth which bore us and sustains us,
the only HOME we shall ever know,
the only paradise we ever *need* —
IF ONLY we had eyes to see.

EDWARD ABBEY

PHOTO BY PAUL NICKLEN

29

Those who have packed far up into GRIZZLY country…
know that the presence of even ONE grizzly on the land
elevates the mountains, DEEPENS the canyons, chills the winds,
brightens the stars, darkens the forests, and quickens the pulse
of ALL who enter it ❧ They know that when a bear DIES,
something **SACRED** in every living thing
interconnected with that realm…*also dies*.

JOHN A. MURRAY

We too need a place to LIVE and thrive ॐ
If you **PROTECT** wild spaces for bears
and learn to live with us,
you are in fact protecting your *own kind.*

JEANIE-BEAR

Coexistence is the language of
RESPECT and **UNDERSTANDING** ∿
Everything else is a bad translation.

SYLVIA DOLSON

Today more than ever before
LIFE must be characterized
by a sense of **UNIVERSAL RESPONSIBILITY**,
not only nation to nation and human to human,
but also human to other forms of life ❧ Life is as *dear*
to the mute CREATURE as it is to a man ❧
Just as one wants happiness and fears pain,
just as one wants to LIVE and not to die,
so do other creatures.

14TH DALAI LAMA

PHOTO BY MICHAEL POLIZA

*W*hen bears SMILE,
the Universe SINGS
in *delight.*

SYLVIA DOLSON

The love for all living creatures
is the most NOBLE attribute of *man.*

CHARLES DARWIN

In all things of NATURE
there is something
of the *marvelous.*

ARISTOTLE

Walk in KINDNESS toward the Earth
and every living being ∾

Without KINDNESS and COMPASSION
for all of Mother Nature's creatures, there can be no true *joy;*
no internal peace, no happiness ∾
Happiness flows from caring for all
sentient beings as if they were
your own FAMILY, because in essence they are ∾
We are all **CONNECTED** to each other
and to the Earth.

SYLVIA DOLSON

PHOTO BY MICHAEL POLIZA

*T*he **SOUL** is the same
in all living creatures,
although the
BODY of each is *different.*

HIPPOCRATES

PHOTO BY DEB POTTS

$\mathcal{W}$hen animals express their *feelings*
they pour out like water
from a spout ∾ Animals' EMOTIONS
are raw, unfiltered, and uncontrolled ∾ Their *joy*
is the purest and most contagious of joys
and their GRIEF the deepest and most devastating ∾
Their PASSIONS bring us to our knees
in delight and sorrow.

MARC BEKOFF

PHOTOS BY SYLVIA DOLSON

50

I believe that there is a
subtle **MAGNETISM** in Nature, which,
if we unconsciously YIELD to it,
will direct us *aright*.

HENRY DAVID THOREAU

$\mathcal{W}$herever you **LIVE** is your *temple,*
if you **TREAT** it like one.

BUDDHA

PHOTOS BY SYLVIA DOLSON

Dance
like nobody is
watching!

Beauty is everywhere,
if you take the time to **LOOK**,
but it BEGINS first of all in the *heart.*

DENNIS FAST

…the *choice* is not
between WILD places or people,
it is between
a RICH or an impoverished
existence for *man*.

THOMAS E. LOVEJOY

PHOTOS BY NIKOLAI ZINOVIEV

Mother Nature is our teacher—
reconnecting us with SPIRIT,
waking us up and liberating our hearts ∾
When we can TRANSCEND our fear
of the creatures of the forest,
then we become ONE with all that is;
we enter a UNITY of existence with our relatives—
the animals, the plants
and the land that *sustains* us.

SYLVIA DOLSON

Being in the presence of BEARS can FEEL wondrously overwhelming—that you are part of a world that is MAGICAL and *sacred*.

SYLVIA DOLSON

PHOTOS BY TONY DATHAN

If you reconnect with nature
and the WILDERNESS
you will not only find the MEANING of life,
but you will experience
what it MEANS to be truly *alive.*

SYLVIA DOLSON

Once we understood the MANNERS we needed to have, their world suddenly OPENED up to *us*.

CHARLIE RUSSELL

PHOTOS BY SYLVIA DOLSON

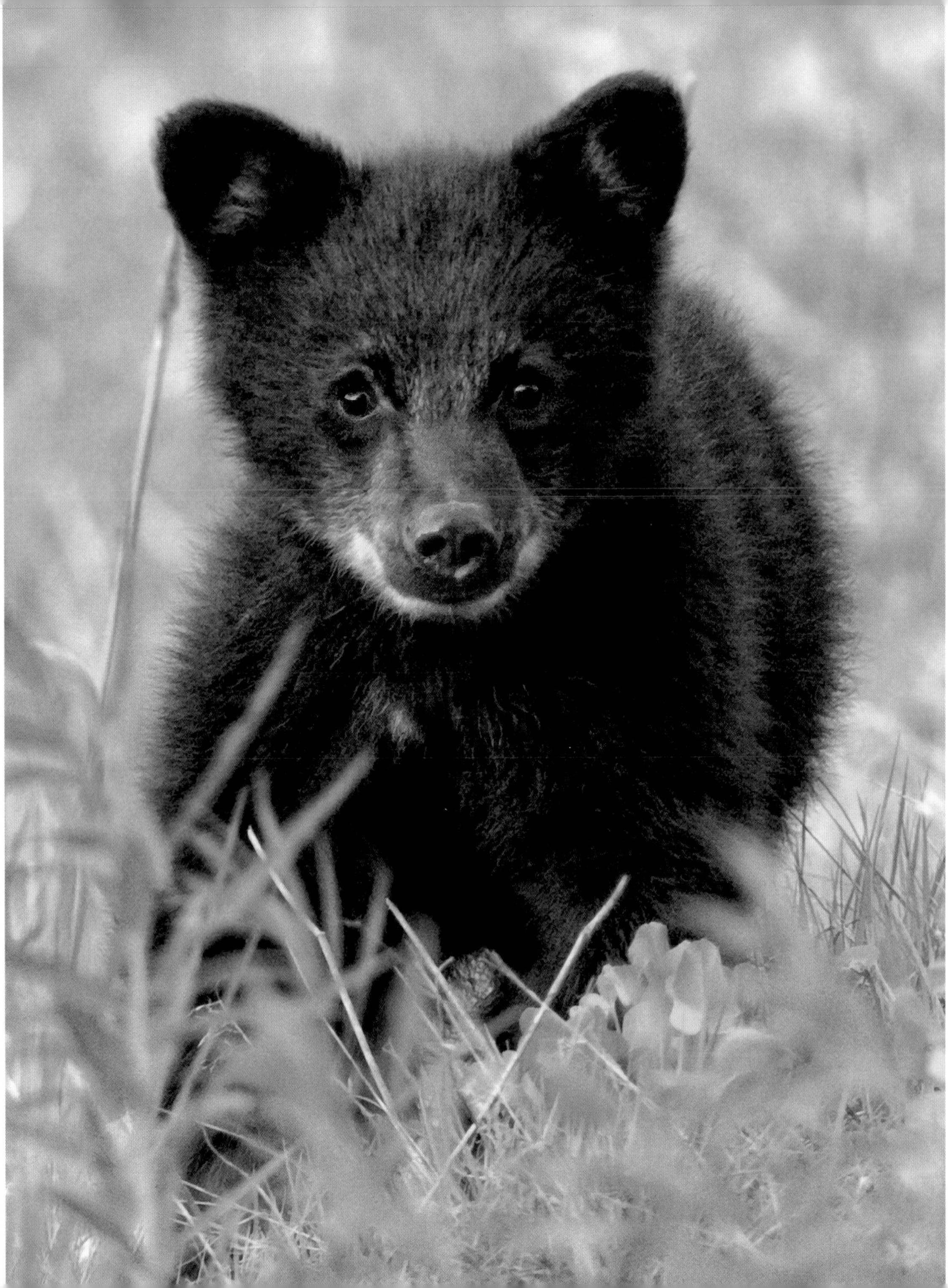

PHOTO BY SYLVIA DOLSON

We should *remember* in our DEALINGS with animals that they are a sacred **TRUST** to us… They cannot speak for themselves.

HARRIET BEECHER STOWE

PHOTO BY JAMES FOUGERE

*T*he BEARS and the wilderness
are your natural INHERITANCE
∾ PROTECT what you *Love.*

SYLVIA DOLSON

PHOTOS BY DEB POTTS

71

PHOTOS BY MICHAEL POLIZA

...just watching an animal closely
can take you OUT of your mind
and bring you into the **PRESENT** moment,
which is where the animal lives
all the time—surrendered to *life.*

ECKHART TOLLE

Only if we UNDERSTAND
can we CARE ∿ Only if we care
will we help ∿ Only if we HELP
shall ALL be *saved*.

JANE GOODALL

PHOTOS BY DEREK KYOSTIA

*$\mathcal{E}$very living BEING
has something to TEACH us—
if we are OPEN to the lesson.*

SYLVIA DOLSON

PHOTOS BY SYLVIA DOLSON

The goal of LIFE
is to make your *heartbeat*
match the **BEAT** of the universe,
to match YOUR nature
with Nature.

JOSEPH CAMPBELL

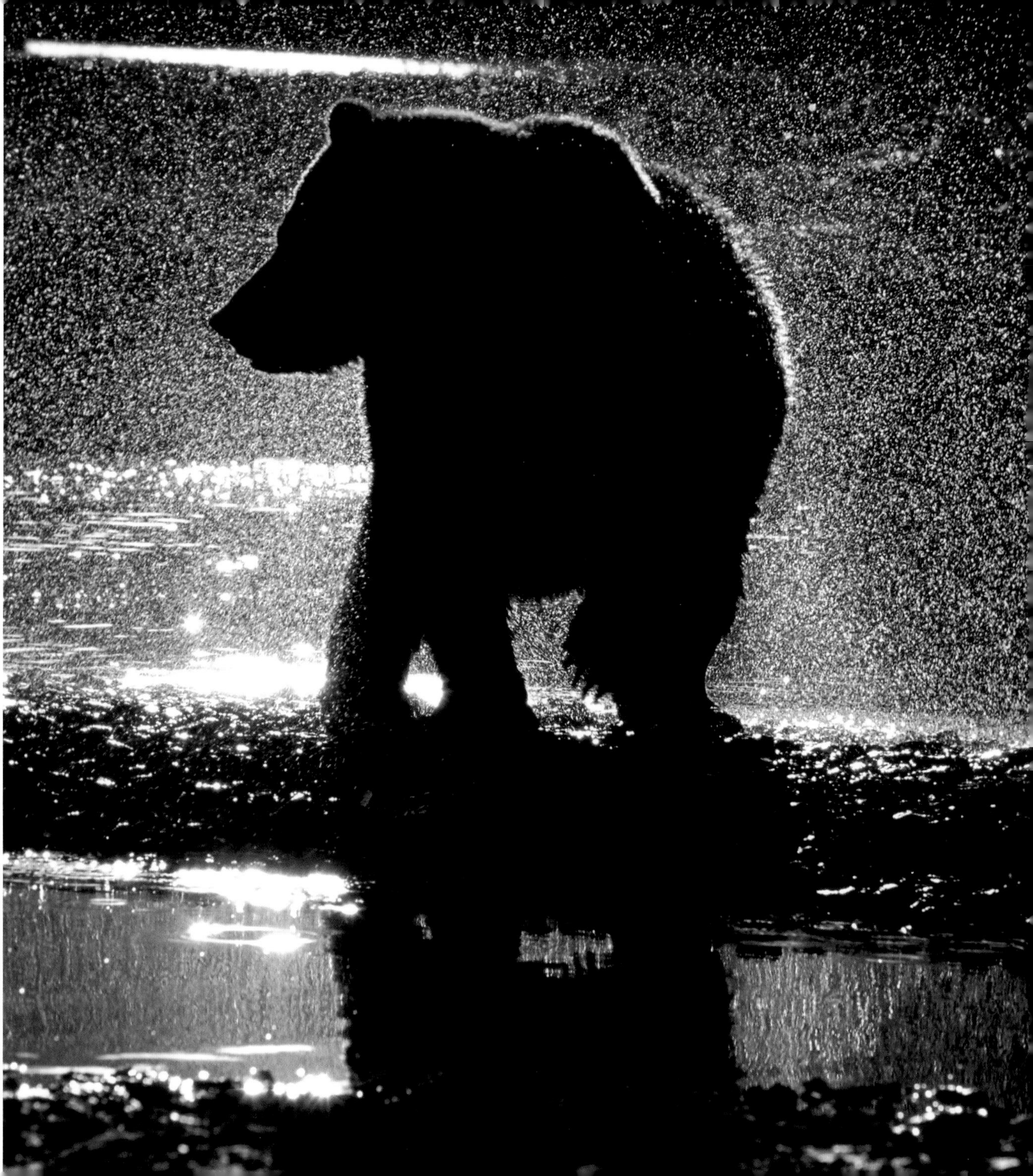

PHOTO BY MATTHIAS BREITER

...practice elementary
COMPASSION
towards our fellow *creatures.*

MAHATMA GANDHI

PHOTOS BY SYLVIA DOLSON

If we can learn to live with bears,
especially the GRIZZLY,
and if we can learn to accommodate
the NEEDS of bears in their natural *environment,*
then maybe we can also find ways
to use the finite **RESOURCES** of our continent
and still maintain some of the DIVERSITY
and NATURAL beauty that were here
when Columbus arrived.

STEVE HERRERO

PHOTOS BY DAVID KRUGHOFF

I am only one, but I am *one*
～ I cannot do everything,
but I can do SOMETHING ～
And I will not let what I cannot do
interfere with what I *can do*.

EDWARD EVERETT HALE

Connecting with the WILDERNESS allows us to live in the flow of a MEANINGFUL, joyful life ❧ Embracing this state of connectedness or *oneness* with other living BEINGS including animals, as opposed to feeling an "otherness" or "separateness" brings a sense of HARMONY and enables us to be at peace with oneself and the *world*.

SYLVIA DOLSON

Bears MATTER
because they are
SENTIENT beings… *like us.*

BARBARA MURRAY

PHOTOS BY SYLVIA DOLSON

$\mathcal{T}$he intuitive knowledge in our HEARTS
allows us to KNOW bears
as gentle and magnificent *beings*.

SYLVIA DOLSON

Nature is inexhaustibly sustainable
IF we CARE for it ❧
It is our universal *responsibility*
to pass a HEALTHY earth
onto future GENERATIONS.

SYLVIA DOLSON

PHOTO BY SYLVIA DOLSON

$\mathcal{I}$'m not an ACTIVIST
because I don't want a revolution ∾
I'm an **ADVOCATE**
because I pray for *evolution*.

MICHAEL HOWIE

PHOTOS BY NIKOLAI ZINOVIEV

Bears are made of the same dust as we,
and BREATHE the same winds
and drink of the same waters ❧ A bear's *days*
are WARMED by the same sun,
his dwellings are overdomed by the same blue sky,
and his LIFE turns and ebbs with
heart-pulsings like ours and was poured
from the same fountain...

JOHN MUIR

PHOTO BY JAMIE DOUGLAS

The *spiritual* journey is the relinquishment,
or unlearning of FEAR,
and the acceptance of LOVE
back into our *hearts.*

MARIANNE WILLIAMSON

PHOTOS BY SYLVIA DOLSON

PHOTO BY MATTIAS BREITER

Each species is a MASTERPIECE,
a **CREATION** assembled
with extreme care and *genius.*

EDWARD O. WILSON

It would be fitting, I think,
if among the LAST manmade tracks on *earth*
could be found the huge **FOOTPRINTS**
of the great BROWN bear.

EARL J. FLEMING

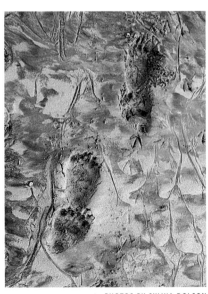

PHOTOS BY SYLVIA DOLSON

PHOTOS BY NIKOLAI ZINOVIEV

Live in WONDER;
manifesting loving-kindness and
COMPASSION ∾ Practice keeping
your heart open to benefit all
sentient beings.

SYLVIA DOLSON

CULTIVATE GENTLE AND PEACEFUL RELATIONSHIPS WITH OTHER BEINGS

LET LOVE GUIDE YOU

Open the conversation to include animals

Make *animals* MATTER

WE MUST GIVE THEM A VOICE

THE BEARS SPEAK

BE KIND *& compassionate* TOWARD ANIMALS

CREATE PEACE

DO THE RIGHT THING

Extend your caring attitude TOWARD THE ENVIRONMENT AND ALL ITS INHABITANTS

PROTECT WHAT YOU LOVE

SYLVIA DOLSON

PHOTO BY SYLVIA DOLSON

Sylvia Dolson

Sylvia Dolson's passion for bears is equaled only by her quest to teach people about the true nature of these wonderful bruins. Her ultimate goal is for a greater coexistence—one in which people and bears live in harmony. As a naturalist, wildlife photographer and freelance writer, Sylvia chooses to spend much of her free time in the company of bears. Having walked among wild black bears, polar bears and grizzlies, she has gained an ever-increasing appreciation and understanding of all the wilderness and its inhabitants.

Sylvia has been involved with the Get Bear Smart Society since 1996 and is now the executive director. She is also a member of the International Association for Bear Research and Management. As a leading expert on living with bears in residential communities, she has been instrumental in bringing forward more progressive, bear-friendly management policies in British Columbia, Canada. She currently co-chairs the Whistler Bear Working Group and was the key catalyst and contributor for Whistler's Black Bear Management Plan. Her persistent hard work and dedication have resulted in establishing Whistler as British Columbia's leading Bear Smart community, becoming a model for others to follow.

PHOTO BY ANASTASIA CHOMLACK

Sylvia travels throughout North America speaking at conferences and workshops. She has authored many reference materials for educational purposes, maintains an extensive website, and writes a regular newspaper column.

Other books include *Bear~ology: Fascinating Facts, Tales & Trivia* and *A Whistler Bear Story*.

Sylvia and her husband, Steve, live in Whistler, British Columbia, where they share their lives with their canine companion, Kia.

To reach Sylvia Dolson, please email info@bear smart.com.

Get Bear Smart Society

The Get Bear Smart Society (GBS), based in Whistler, British Columbia, is a registered Canadian charity that works hard to ensure people and bears safely and respectfully coexist. GBS has helped create a paradigm shift in people's attitudes toward bears and other wildlife by replacing fear and misunderstanding with respect and understanding.

The Society's goal is to minimize the number of bears killed as a result of human-caused problems. They accomplish this by helping the public prevent conflict at their homes, work and play; championing policymakers to create Bear Smart communities; and encouraging police and bear managers to choose non-lethal bear management options.

Visit www.bearsmart.com to learn more about living conflict-free with bears, staying safe while recreating and working in bear country; as well as creating Bear Smart communities and using bear-friendly management policies.

Please consider making a donation today and investing in a future that not only includes bears, but considers their needs and welfare along with people's.

Get Bear Smart Society
P.O. Box 502, Whistler, BC
Canada VON 1BO
www.bearsmart.com
email: info@bearsmart.com

Writers and Photographers

Abbey, Edward Paul (1927–1989) was an American author and essayist noted for his advocacy of environmental issues, criticism of public land policies, and anarchist political views.

Aristotle (384–322 BCE) was a Greek philosopher and polymath, a student of Plato and teacher of Alexander the Great. He is recognized as one of the most important founders of Western philosophy.

Balcombe, Dr. Jonathan is an American author, animal behavior expert and passionate advocate for animals and their living spaces. www.jonathanbalcombe.com

Bekoff, Dr. Marc is an American teacher, prolific writer and lectures internationally on issues of animal behavior, cognitive ethology, and compassionate conservation. www.marcbekoff.com

Breiter, Matthias is an internationally renowned author, cinematographer, wildlife photographer and biologist (specializing in bears). German-born, living in Canada and Alaska, Matthias is also deeply involved with conservation efforts in the Arctic and Subarctic. www.breiterphoto.com

Buber, Martin (1878–1965) was an Austrian-born Jewish "existentialist" philosopher.

Buddha or Siddhartha Gautama Buddha (563–483 BCE) was a spiritual teacher from the Indian subcontinent, on whose teachings Buddhism was founded.

Campbell, Joseph (1904–1987) was an American mythologist, writer and lecturer. His work is vast, covering many aspects of the human experience.

Dalai Lama, named Tenzin Gyatso, is the 14th and current Dalai Lama, head monk of the Gelugpa lineage of Tibetan Buddhism and Nobel Peace Prize winner.

Darwin, Charles (1809–1882) was an English naturalist, famous for proposing a theory of evolution contrary to the popular view of other naturalists at the time, namely natural selection.

Dathan, Tony is a Canadian who has photographed people and wildlife for over 20 years, but has a soft spot for North American bears. www.tdphotos.ca

Dolson, Sylvia (see page 108).

Douglas, Jamie is a Scottish-born Canadian wildlife conservation photographer with a passion for black bears. www.jamiedouglasphotography.com

Fast, Dennis is one of Manitoba's premier wildlife photographers. His photos have appeared in many books and calendars. Dennis has presented at a variety of events, workshops, and seminars across Canada. www.dennisfast.com

Fleming, Earl was an American teacher who also worked for Alaska Fish & Game in the 1950s.

Fougere, James is a Canadian avid photographer and outdoor enthusiast who also runs intimate bear and

scenic tours in the Whistler, BC area. www.Whistler
DiscoveryTours.com

Gandhi, Mahatma (1869–1948) was the preeminent leader of Indian nationalism in British-ruled India. Employing non-violent civil disobedience, Gandhi led India to independence and inspired movements for non-violence, civil rights and freedom across the world.

Goodall, Dr. Jane is a British primatologist, Dame of the British Empire, and UN Messenger of Peace. Considered to be the world's foremost expert on chimpanzee behavior, she is also the founder of the Jane Goodall Institute and has worked extensively on conservation and animal welfare issues. To learn more about Dr. Goodall and the Institute, please visit www.jane goodall.org.

Hale, Edward Everett (1822–1909) was an American author, historian and Unitarian clergyman.

Herrero, Dr. Steve is a Canadian and leading authority on bear ecology, behaviour, conservation and management, as well as author of *Bear Attacks: Their Causes and Avoidance*.

Hippocrates (460–370 BCE) was an ancient Greek physician of the Age of Pericles, and is considered one of the most outstanding figures in the history of medicine.

Howie, Michael is an international award-winning Canadian journalist who has taken his sharp eye for crime reporting and focused it on the environment. www.ihowie.ca

Hunter, Linda Jo is an American guide, tracker, naturalist and writer, often expressing her love of wildlife in art. Hunter is an advocate for animal habitat preservation and the welfare of wild bears.

Jeanie-Bear (1991–2011) was an iconic black bear who lived in Whistler, BC. Her immediate family included 14 cubs from seven litters. Jeanie was one of those extraordinary bears who will be forever remembered as an ambassador for her kind. She was laid to rest in her home range on Whistler Mountain. www.bearsmart.com/Jeanie

Krughoff, David is a Canadian wildlife photographer and author, passionate about saving wildlife and habitat. www.krugyandkrugy.com

Kyostia, Derek is a Canadian biologist, interpretative guide and photographer, dedicating his time between the grizzly bears of coastal British Columbia, the polar bears of the Arctic and the penguins of Antarctica.

Lovejoy, Thomas E. is an American tropical and conservation biologist working in the Brazilian Amazon. He is one of the main protagonists for the science and conservation of biological diversity.

Lynch, Wayne is a Canadian naturalist, wildlife photographer and award-winning science writer, as well as a popular guest lecturer. www.waynelynch.ca

Muir, John (1838–1914) was a Scottish-born American naturalist, author, and early advocate of preservation of wilderness in the United States.

Murray, Barbara is a Canadian advocate for bears and founder of Bears Matter, working to help six of the eight bear species around the world. www.bears matter.com

Murray, John A. is an American award-winning nature writer and editor of numerous nature anthologies including "The Great Bear".

Nicklen, Paul is a Canadian biologist and internationally acclaimed wildlife photographer; but prefers to call himself an interpreter and a translator, using his images to get people's attention to raise awareness for conservation efforts. www.paulnicklen.com

Poliza, Michael is a German entrepreneur, expedition leader, travel experience designer, best-selling author and award-winning wildlife and landscape photographer. www.michaelpoliza.com

Potts, Deb is an American who travels the world seeking adventure, magic and the occasional Truth, and has found all three in bears.

Rogers, Dr. Lynn is an American wildlife research biologist who has been studying black bears for 46 years. Rogers founded the North American Black Bear Center, in Ely, Minnesota to educate the public on the true nature of bears. www.bear.org

Rumi, Jalal ad-Din Muhammad (1207–1273) was a Persian poet, jurist, theologian, and Sufi mystic.

Russell, Charlie is a Canadian rancher and author who has spent much of his life studying bears in the wild to help people better understand their true nature. www.charlierussellbears.com

Seattle, Chief (1780–1866) was a Dkhw'Duw'Absh (Duwamish) chief, respected by his people and widely known for his speech in favour of the environment and native American land rights.

Stowe, Harriet Beecher (1811–1896) was an American social activist and author most famous for her anti-slavery novel *Uncle Tom's Cabin*.

Thoreau, Henry David (1817–1862) was an American author, poet, philosopher, abolitionist, naturalist, tax resister, development critic, surveyor, historian, and leading transcendentalist.

Tolle, Eckhart, a German born, Canadian resident, is a spiritual teacher, best-selling author and sought after public speaker. www.eckharttolle.com

Williams, Anthony Douglas is a Canadian who has spent many years studying numerical patterns and mysterious phenomena. Much of what he has learned is revealed in his book: *Inside the Divine Pattern*. www.divinepattern.com

Williamson, Marianne is an internationally acclaimed American spiritual author and lecturer. Her teachings are based on *A Course in Miracles*. www.marianne.com

Wilson, Edward O. is an American biologist, researcher, theorist, naturalist and author. He is known as "the father of sociobiology". www.eowilsonfoundation.org

Zinoviev, Nikolai is a freelance wildlife photographer from Moscow, Russia whose mission is to bring wildlife into people's homes and workplaces through his photographs. www.nikzinoviev.com

Sources for Bios: Wikipedia.com, authors of quotes, their representatives, or their websites.